HOCKEY THE NHL® WAY
Goaltending

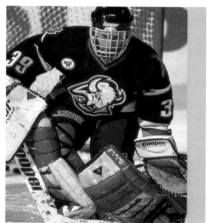
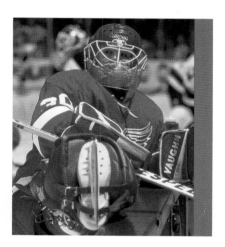

Sean Rossiter

GREYSTONE BOOKS
Douglas & McIntyre
Vancouver/Toronto

In memory of Terry Sawchuk: four shutouts, eight straight victories, and the 1952 Stanley Cup championship with Detroit.

Copyright © 1997 by Sean Rossiter

97 98 99 00 01   5 4 3 2 1

Greystone Books
A division of Douglas & McIntyre Ltd.
1615 Venables Street
Vancouver, British Columbia
Canada V5L 2H1

Canadian Cataloguing in Publication Data
Rossiter, Sean, 1946 –
    Hockey, the NHL way: goaltending

    ISBN 1-55054-549-3

    1. Hockey—Goalkeeping—Juvenile literature. I. Title.
GV848.76.R68 1997   j796.962'27   C97-910320-7

Editing by Anne Rose, Kerry Banks
Cover and text design by Peter Cocking
Instructional photographs: Stefan Schulhof/Schulhof Photography
Front cover photograph: *Patrick Roy* by John Giamundo/Bruce Bennett Studios
Back cover photographs by Bruce Bennett Studios. Photographers:
    Curtis Joseph: John Tremmel • *Ed Belfour:* John Giamundo •
    Martin Brodeur, Dominik Hasek: Claus Andersen • *Mike Richter:* Scott Levy •
    Chris Osgood: Michael Digirolamo
Printed and bound in Canada by Friesens
Printed on acid-free paper

Every reasonable care has been taken to trace the ownership of copyrighted visual material. Information that will enable the publisher to rectify any reference or credit is welcome.

The publisher gratefully acknowledges the assistance of the Canada Council for the Arts and of the British Columbia Ministry of Tourism, Small Business and Culture.

Contents

The NHL Way team

Our players

Brandon Hart

Kendall Trout

Michelle Marsz

Jesse Birch

Daniel Birch

Jordan Sengara

Nicolas Fung

Will Harvey

Tyler Dietrich

Rob Tokawa

Scott Tupper

Brian Melnyk

Special thanks

Young goaltenders have special parents who get them to the rink early, console them after bad games and mortgage the house to keep them equipped. Thanks also to David McConnachie, director of publishing for the NHL; to Chris Brumwell and Devin Smith of the Vancouver Canucks; to Rick Noonan and the staff at the UBC Thunderbird Winter Sports Centre; and to Mike Harling of Sportsbook Plus. Todd Ewen of the San Jose Sharks is, as always, a valued friend of this project.

Our coaching advisory staff

Paul Carson
Coach coordinator, the British Columbia Amateur Hockey Association

An assistant coach of the UBC Thunderbirds, Paul Carson is also the provincial coach coordinator responsible for coach development programs in B.C. He is a master course conductor for the NCCP, and coached high school hockey in Sendai, Japan. He recently completed work on the CHA Hockey Curriculum series.

Jack Cummings
Hockey coordinator, the Hollyburn Country Club

Jack Cummings played goal for four years at both the Junior A level and with the University of Alberta. He was an assistant coach to the U of A's legendary Clare Drake for six years, and has been hockey coordinator at the Hollyburn Country Club in West Vancouver for four years.

Bill Holowaty
Minor hockey coach

Still the third-highest scorer in UBC Thunderbird history, Bill Holowaty played and coached professionally and worked as a hockey school instructor in Japan for seven years. He played for Canada's gold-medal team at the World University Games in 1982, and on Canada's first Spengler Cup winners of 1985.

Ken Melnyk
Author, the Hockey Skills Development Program, Tykes/Atoms

Named coach of the year (1995–96) by the B.C. Amateur Hockey Association, Ken Melnyk was on the organizing committee for the 1988 Winter Olympics. He wrote the Games' deficit-free business plan. However, Ken's most notable achievement may be Brian Melnyk, one of our NHL Way players.

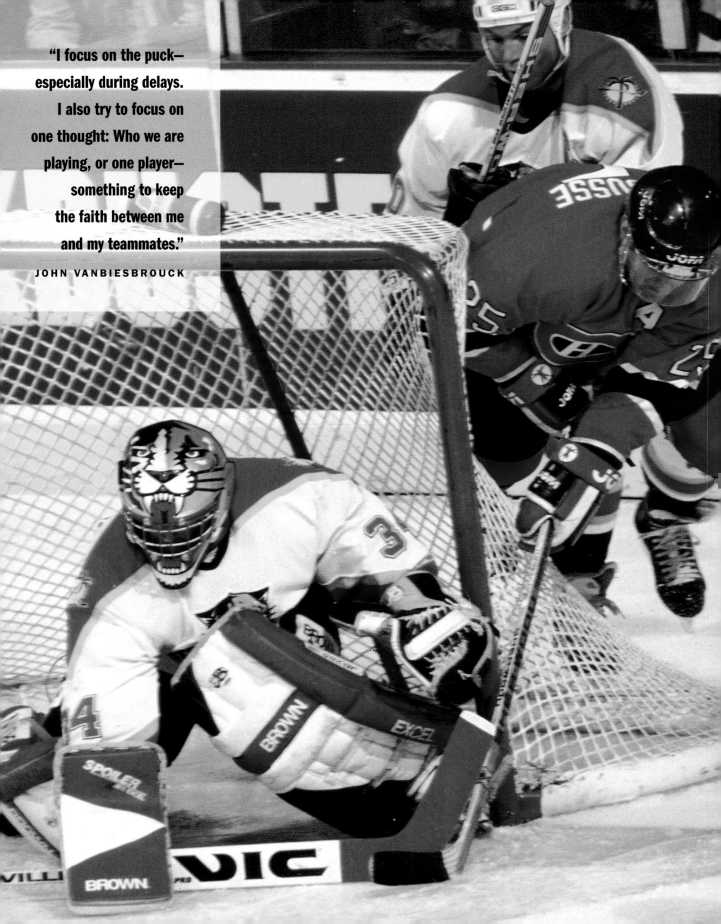

"I focus on the puck—
especially during delays.
I also try to focus on
one thought: Who we are
playing, or one player—
something to keep
the faith between me
and my teammates."

JOHN VANBIESBROUCK

Foreword

There is no better feeling in team sports than keeping your hockey club in a tight game, making save after save, slamming the door on your opponents. But like anything special, doing this job isn't easy.

Coaches know that the goalie is the key player on a team. Goalies can win games almost by themselves—and lose them, too. It takes a special person to be a goaltender: tough, dependable and willing to learn.

No one can tell you exactly how to play goal. No one cares how you stop the puck—as long as you stop it. So this book does not try to make you play one way; most goalies combine moves from different overall styles. In this book, when a basic skill is done differently by stand-up or butterfly goalies, *Goaltending* explains it both ways. Take those tips that seem right for you. Try new moves in practice. Do what feels natural.

You already know that good goaltending depends as much on your attitude as on how you play. How you deal with being scored on is the most important aspect of being a good goaltender. Even the best goaltenders make three or four mistakes a game. This book is filled with tips on how to learn from the bad games every goalie experiences.

It's a funny thing about goaltending—and life, for that matter. If we learn how to handle failure, success is often right around the corner.

Brian Burke
Senior vice-president and director of hockey operations
NHL Enterprises

Introduction

When Kirk McLean of the Vancouver Canucks was asked for a goaltending tip for this book, he answered with two words: "Have fun."

That wasn't what we were expecting to hear. Captain Kirk plays goal by the book: he's called a stand-up goalie, and most of the time he plays on his feet. Yet he makes half of his saves from the butterfly position. The idea was to find out how he learned to handle the puck so well. Or when, exactly, a goalie should leave his or her feet. Or maybe how he stays on such an even keel—never down on himself, never too high.

But no-o-o. Instead, McLean tells young goalies to have fun out there. Haven't we heard that before? Of course. But wait. Just a moment here. Isn't it true? Doesn't every goalie want to have fun? Sure. Yet a lot of us don't. We all know that.

"There's enough pressure put on you that you tend to overlook the fun aspects of the game," says McLean.

Now isn't *that* the truth?

Not only do we let others put pressure on us, we do it to ourselves. We don't even want to look as if we're having fun. Smile? Then go out and give up five goals? Are you kidding?

McLean says that when you aren't having fun, the best part of being on a team gets lost. You stop being part of the team. You go into a shell. Now, there's no doubt that goal-tenders enjoy the game more when they feel they are playing well. Winning makes it fun. The real test comes when you lose.

Are you going to mope around, feeling sorry for yourself? Are you?

As a goaltender, how well you play depends on how well you prepare. There is no time to get ready once the puck drops.

NHL goaltenders will tell you that the mental aspects of playing this demanding position are more important than how you move in the net. Many great athletes don't make it as goalies at the top level; watching them play, you wonder how some star goaltenders do it.

Work out a routine that begins at least a couple of hours before the game—one that gets you relaxed and in the right frame of mind *before* you step on the ice for your warmup. And remember, your warmup doesn't get you ready to play. It's just the finishing touch to your pregame routine.

BEFORI

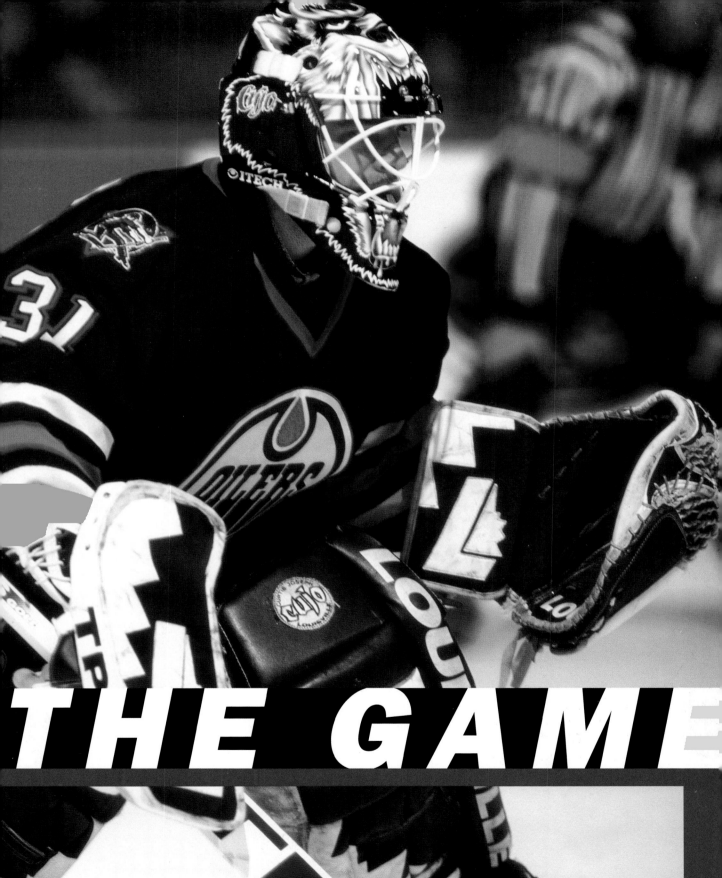

THE GAME

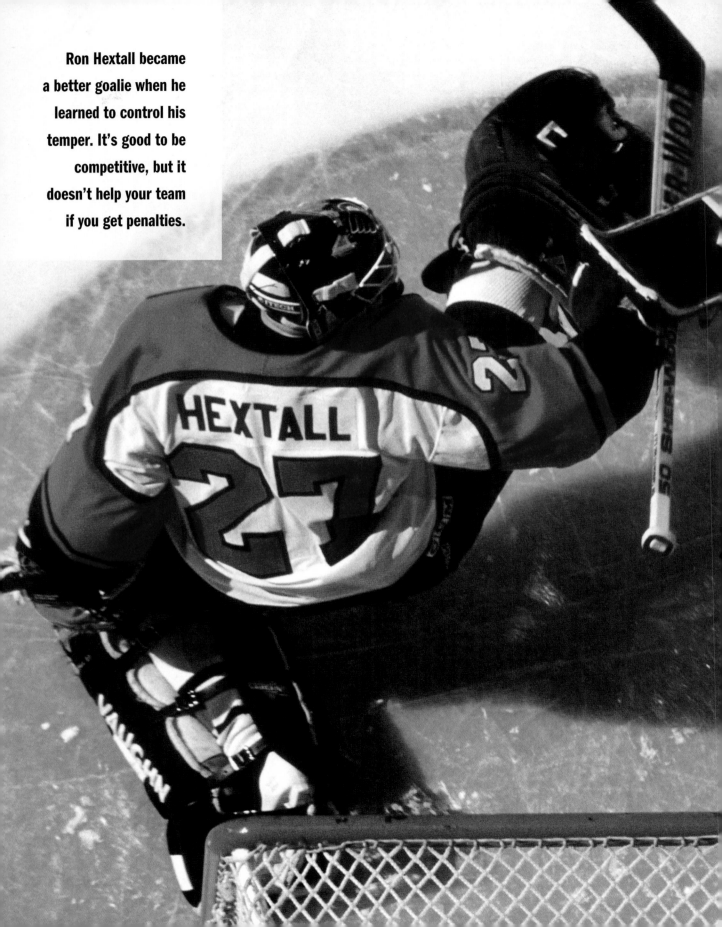

Ron Hextall became a better goalie when he learned to control his temper. It's good to be competitive, but it doesn't help your team if you get penalties.

How you get the job done on the ice is up to you. But there are some important habits that good goalies have in common.

Good goalies are competitive

Patrick Roy has been called the ultimate competitor. That means he hates to do less than his best—at anything.

Good goalies are always learning

Jacques Plante won five straight Stanley Cups, partly because he learned from every game by studying his opposing goalie—good or bad. That means being in the game, even when the puck is at the other end.

Good goalies are responsible

Take care of your equipment. Take care of your teammates by correcting their mistakes. Never blame anyone else for a goal. Never stay down after a goal to show you had no chance.

Good goalies are organized

Develop a pregame routine. Learn what you have to do to play well, and stick to that. Begin a couple of hours before the game, alone and at home, by visualizing the great saves you'll make. Stretch before you go to the rink; the dressing room is no place to spend time on the floor. Be in the dressing room at least 45 minutes before the game. Be there first. Take your time dressing.

Good goalies are consistent

Every goalie likes to make big saves, but nothing is more of a letdown for your teammates than watching you miss easy shots and showboat on difficult ones. You don't want your opponents to think they can score on any shot. Make them earn their goals. Be steady. For any goalie, consistency is the key to moving up in the world of hockey.

The goaltender's code

Concentrate

Depending on how you rate your opponents, you might start worrying about an upcoming game days ahead. It's healthy to be concerned about how you will play. It means you care. But worrying doesn't help. Channel all that energy and get it working for you. Use it to focus and concentrate on the game—starting a few hours before the referee drops the puck.

Visualize

A few hours before you step on the ice, begin visualizing yourself making saves. Start getting ready for the impact of the puck by *feeling* it hit you. You have the angle right, so the puck always hits you. Next, start extending the movements you are imagining. Feel yourself turning low shots into the corners with your stick and feet, or flexing your knees as you rise to take high shots off your chest. Finally, use your imagination to put yourself in the game, anticipating plays.

Pregame routine

Imagine yourself making big saves: high shots, low shots, dekes, breakaways.

Be at the rink early. Check your equipment. Give yourself time to put it on right.

Be prepared

You wear more equipment than any other team-game player, so give yourself lots of time to put it on right. Rushing when you're dressing means loose buckles and straps under your skate-blades, and you know when you will discover them. You will be first on the ice, so be the first dressed—always.

Warmup

Work hard in the warmup. This is the place and time to work into a rhythm: find a groove and be ready for a two-on-one or a breakaway off the opening faceoff. Expect either. Some goalies, such as Kirk McLean of the Canucks, use the rock music at the warmup to get their bodies moving to a beat. Finding the right tempo can carry you through the game.

Warmup guidelines

- Your teammates need to take it easy with their first shots. Have them hit you in the pads, *before* they shoot at the lower corners.
- There is no excuse for your teammates to shoot high in the warmup. The warmup is for you, the goalie, not for your team's shooters to practise roofing the puck. Remember, players who shoot high often believe they are warming up your hands. But your hands don't need warming up—your feet do.

> **N H L   T I P**
> "Part of my warmup routine includes an intensive stretch—it allows me to be nice and loose to prevent any muscle pulls."
> **G R A N T   F U H R**

Easy shots at first. Work on doing it right in the warmup. Watch the puck into your glove.

Start making the puck your focus. React to it, let it guide you, and then start controlling rebounds. Be in command.

The warmup

No goalie steps onto the ice ready to make saves with his or her feet, and that's where most shots come.

- Don't allow your teammates to skate in and shoot when others are shooting from the blueline. Limit the number of pucks.
- Never allow your teammates to deke you when you're cold—unless they want a goalie with a strained groin muscle.

You can't be thinking about each move during a game. Everything you do has to be instinctive. You see the puck, you stop it. It's as simple as that.

For your movements in the net to become habits, you have to practise until they become second nature. Some goalies don't like practising—why collect bruises with no points on the line? Here's why: There's no time to think with the puck on your doorstep and a game to be won. There's an old saying in sports that luck comes from preparation. Great saves often *look* lucky, but how you practise is how you play.

Once the game begins, stop thinking and react. Focus. Make stopping the puck your only task in life.

I N T

E N E T

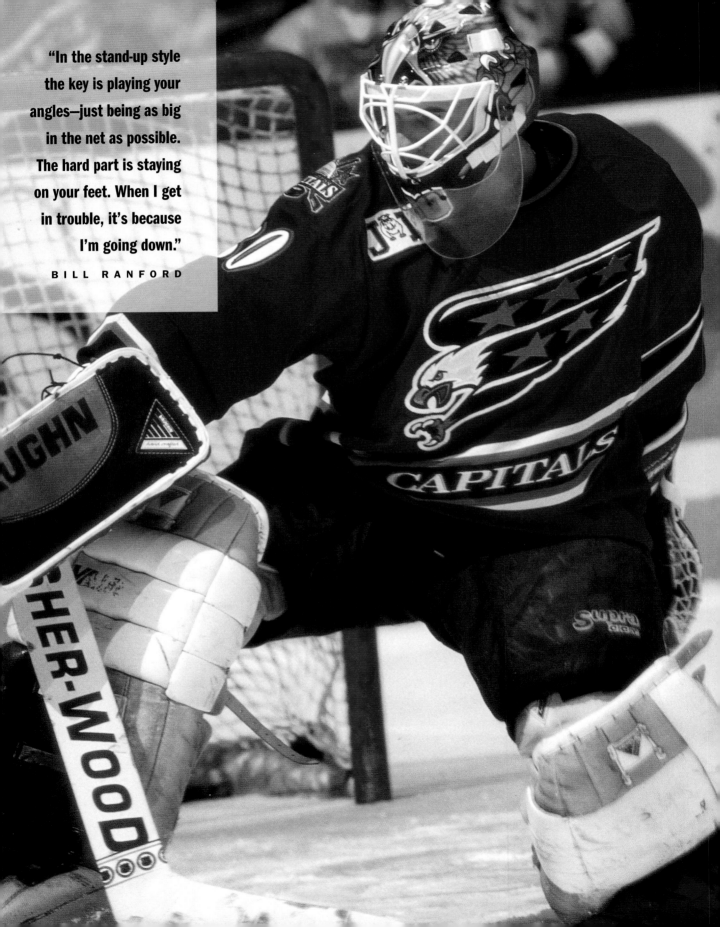

"In the stand-up style the key is playing your angles—just being as big in the net as possible. The hard part is staying on your feet. When I get in trouble, it's because I'm going down."

BILL RANFORD

Styles in goaltending come and go. Goalies usually develop their own unique style by finding out what works best for them, and by watching other netminders. Most goalies, however, play a combination of two basic styles: stand-up and butterfly.

Stand-up

The classic high-percentage style, stand-up goaltending requires good footwork to move sideways. Even a stand-up goalie like Kirk McLean goes to his knees to make half of his saves. Other stand-up goalies: Bill Ranford, Jeff Hackett.
Strengths: Less of a five-hole; good lateral and in-and-out movement; best for controlling rebounds.
Weaknesses: Lower corners uncovered; screen shots can be a problem; angles must be perfect.

T I P
"When I play with men's teams, I play more of a stand-up style. With women's hockey there are a lot more scrambles in front of the net, so I play a butterfly style."
D A N I E L L E   D U B É
Goaltender, Canadian Women's National Hockey Team

Brandon shows his stand-up stance: feet shoulder-width apart, back fairly straight.

Kendall's knees are close together, feet wide apart: a classic butterfly stance.

Styles

Butterfly

This style gets its name from the way some goalies go to their knees with pads spread outward to cover most of the goalmouth ice surface. Tom Barrasso, Patrick Roy and Andy Moog are butterfly goalies who have won Stanley Cups.
Strengths: A good style against screen shots or low deflections; good for freezing the puck—you are already down.
Weaknesses: Timing is important. When you go to your knees, you can't move with the play; pad saves create rebounds in front; shooters will go high on you.

The ready position

As a goaltender, all your moves start with you standing still. If your stance, or ready position, is not right, making the proper moves will be difficult, or impossible. For example, if your ready position doesn't allow you to keep your stickblade on the ice, you will give up bad goals no matter what else you do.

What to do

No matter which style you play, you have to be in the ready position and in the right place *before* the puck arrives. Doing the splits or reaching with your catcher look good, but either move means you were out of position.

You want to be as big in the net as you can be. That means being square to the puck, on the shot line, with your stickblade

Stance

Many goalies bend too much at the waist. Bend at the knees and keep your upper body up, so the puck can hit it.

Your stance should be relaxed. Flex your knees to keep your stickblade on the ice.

> **TIP**
>
> In the ready position, don't bend over from the waist. Flex your knees, not your hips. Keep your back as straight as possible.

flat on the ice. Most problems in goaltending come from failures in one or more of these three areas.

Your biggest pieces of equipment are your leg pads and upper-body protector. Your ready position must make the most of these big pads. So think about how you sit in a chair: your lower legs and chest are almost vertical. Then think of yourself as sitting in the ready position—without the chair, of course—with your lower legs and chest available for the puck to hit. That's the way to cover the most net. You'll feel the strain in the big muscles of your thighs.

Stance checklist

The rest of the ready position depends on your style. Try some of these ideas:

- Improve your side-to-side balance by keeping your hands level with each other.
- Remember, every shot comes from ice level. The closer the shooter, the more likely the shot will come in low. Also, it's easier to lift your catching glove than lower it.
- Keep both gloves in front of your body. That will help you see every shot right into your glove and keep the puck in front of you. Another advantage of keeping your hands out front is that, as you are seen by the shooter, the gaps between your body and your arms will close. This makes you look more solid.
- One sign of a good goalie is when you see very little movement.

T I P

Most goals are scored against goalies who are out of their stance.

Holding your gloves level helps keep you balanced.

When your gloves are ahead of your body, the gaps between your arms and body close, and it's easier to see the puck into your gloves.

Stance

The puck hits good goalies just as it finds the sticks of good scorers. It's all a matter of angles.

- Felix Potvin knows that even butterfly goalies need to play their angles. You may be covering more of the ice surface, but you can't move much once you are down.
- Know how the elbow on your stick side feels with your stick-blade flat on the ice—in both positions, on your feet and in the butterfly. Patrick Roy makes sure he has his hands up when he's on his knees.

GARTH SNOW ▶

Good footwork is the key to movement and balance. No matter which style you use—stand-up, butterfly or a combination—footwork is critical.

Stand-up

As a stand-up goalie, your footwork will be more complicated than for the other styles. Why? You'll be on your feet more of the time.

In the ready position, a stand-up goalie's feet are shoulder-width or a little more apart. You might lean forward to get low, but to make the kick save on low shots to the corner, balance on the balls of your feet, with your toes slightly outward. You can then quickly get your foot sideways and in front of the puck, with your stickblade in front of it for more protection and rebound control.

Footwork

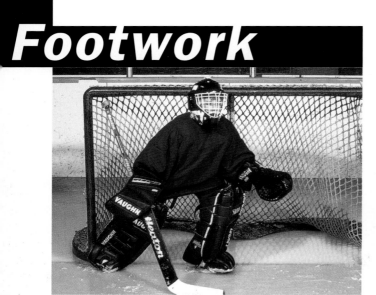

To get across faster, the T-push is the ticket. Keep your stick on the ice. Push off with your back foot.

Turning the puck into the corner on the stick side is a key stand-up skill. Practise it.

Leg kick: Set your off-side skate and push toward the side the shot is aimed at. Transfer your weight, kick with your toe outward, and move your stick with the kicking foot.

Side to side: For a stand-up goalie, the side-to-side move starts like the leg kick. Set your off-side skate, transfer your weight to the skate on the side you want to move toward, turn the foot on that side outward, and glide. This is called a T-push. To stop, lean back and, still facing forward, use the push-off skate as a brake.

Butterfly

As a butterfly goalie, you lean forward on the balls of your feet, and grip the ice with your skateblade toes. In the ready position, your feet are wider apart than in the stand-up style. Because your knees are close together and your feet wide apart, this stance is often called the inverted-V. Footwork is easy for butterfly goalies because their feet are almost always pointed straight ahead.

Up and down: With your front skateblade tips as an anchor, drop to your knees with your feet spread wide.

Protecting the five-hole: To close off the five-hole, try to make the tops of your pads touch. Learn to rise and fall with your stickblade flat on the ice by opening and closing your stick-side elbow.

N H L   T I P

"The key thing I learned from Russian goalie Vladislav Tretiak was to be a top-conditioned goaltender. You have to be very flexible, and work on developing strong quads and a strong back."
E D   B E L F O U R

Shuffle across the goalmouth in short sideways steps, keeping track of the play.

Brandon moves to his right without losing his stance.

Closing the five-hole and raising your gloves are important in the butterfly.

Footwork

Regain your feet by digging your skateblade toes into the ice and by pushing down with the insides of your feet. Feel the strain on your inner thighs—these muscles are a butterfly goalie's motor. Take care of them.

Patrick Roy says that most of his exercise program focuses on the lower part of his body. For you, that means running, squats (not too deep), leg extensions and, most important, lots of stretching—for both the front and back of your thighs.

Always keep your stickblade flat on the ice. As you move from side to side, stay square to the puck so your stickblade remains on the ice. Keep some downward pressure on your stickblade. Keep your stickblade a foot or so ahead of your toes, to absorb the force of the shot.

Stand-up

While remaining in the ready position, move your stick back and forth in front of you. The blade will make an arc on the ice. It will also be angled back toward you—especially at the sides.

When you make saves on low shots to your sides, the puck will be deflected off your stick to the corners, or up and out of the rink. You can learn to control where the rebounds go. An advantage of the stand-up style is being able to control rebounds on shots to the lower corners.

Using your stick

A stand-up goalie can cover the entire goalmouth with the stick. Outside the posts, it can deflect shots away.

Butterfly goalies cover most of the goalmouth ice surface. The stick covers the five-hole.

Butterfly

For a butterfly goalie, the stickblade's role is to stop shots aimed at the five-hole. When a butterfly goalie is in the ready position, his or her feet are wider apart than a stand-up goalie's feet would be. The stick covers most of that opening, but not all of it.

It is not easy to keep the stickblade on the ice while you are dropping into the butterfly or springing back to your feet. But that is when your five-hole is most at risk.

By being in line with the shooter, a goalie covers as much of the net as possible. Being on the line a shot must travel to enter the centre of the net is called "playing the angle."

Position is everything when you're a goalie. You must know where the puck will go before it is shot and be waiting in the ready position. In other words, you must anticipate the play. There are two aspects to playing angles: side-to-side movements and gliding in and out of the net. The key is to move ahead, back or sideways without losing your ready position.

Nothing about goaltending is easy, but moving around while keeping square to the shooter and in your stance is the biggest step you can take toward being a reliable goalie.

MOV

When the puck is far away from the net, move out. As the puck moves to one side, back up toward the net and to that side. Or, if a lone shooter comes in on the wing, move out to challenge the shooter. If no shot comes, start moving back into the net as the shooter passes the circle hash marks—in case the shooter tries to go around you. Think of yourself as being attached to your posts by big elastic bands. Move with the play. The puck controls you.

How to do it

A goalie glides in and out with small movements of the ankles and feet. That is why goaltenders have to be good skaters. They must move around the ice as quickly as other players, but without using their bodies for leverage. All the power is generated from the knees down.

In & out

Kendall's solid stance and correct angle on the puck allows her to cover a lot of the net from inside the crease . . .

. . . but she covers almost all of it by coming out on a line with the puck. Go for the top corner? She dares you.

T I P

Come out to play the shot, then *back in* to play the deke.

Ian Young, a respected goaltending coach, calls the in-and-out movement "telescoping." As you move toward the shooter, you get bigger and block more of the net.

As with every rule in goaltending, there is an exception. If an opposition player appears to either side of you, you must cheat back to the net and a bit toward that side. Sometimes goalies have to do two things at once. You still focus on the shooter, as always. Don't be distracted. Stay on the line of the shot. Stopping the shot is still your main job. But be ready to react to the pass.

So far we've been talking about the simplest situation: goalie versus shooter. But what if the shooter passes to a teammate? Try stacking your pads. Throwing yourself feet-first across the goalmouth makes a great save against two or more opponents.

How to do it

Push off the same way you would in a T-push, then flex the knee you push off with. Lead with the pad on the side you are moving toward. Concentrate on getting the push-off pad—the lower pad as you cross the goalmouth—flat on the ice fast. Don't fall on your bottom elbow. That keeps your upper body off the ice, and it's hard on your elbows.

Your stick is important. If stacking to your stick side, hold it above your top pad, adding to the goalmouth area you have

> **T I P**
> The key is to get as as much of the ice surface covered as soon as possible. Get that lower pad down flat. Then get your upper body down—fast.

Because a goalie has both glove and stick sides, stacking the pads is a bit different each way.

Either way, Kendall is blocking the low shot and any possible pass across the goalmouth.

Stacking the pads

covered. When stacking to your glove side, get the wide part of your stick flat on the ice to cover the surface as your body falls.

Finish with your body flat across the goalmouth. Often a pass receiver at the open side will deflect the puck back toward the middle of the goalmouth, figuring your body will be the last part of you on the ice. Get everything down fast!

Resist the urge to kick out to show yourself you've made the save. That creates a rebound. Usually the puck will be under you. Just wait. Listen. You'll soon know if you made the save.

Andy Moog is a butterfly goalie who plays at the top of his crease and stays on his feet a lot. Here, he directs a rebound to the corner by turning it with his stick in textbook style.

Goaltending is based on reactions. You react to the play because there isn't time to think in the net. Well-chosen drills simulate game situations. By doing drills over and over again, goalies develop the right reactions to a variety of situations.

Five-point drill

First, pick a player to be the "coach." The goalies then face the "coach." With a stick, the "coach" points left, right, forward or backward. Goalies move in the direction indicated until the direction changes. Be careful to maintain your stance throughout the drill.

A variation is to add up and down movements. The "coach" points a stickblade up or down and shouts "Hit the deck!" Work on getting back up fast.

Post-to-post

A passer has the puck behind the net. That player can pass from either side of the net into the slot, or put the puck on the net if you're not at the post fast enough. Try to block the pass with your stick.

Post-to-slot

A passer is behind the goal line, 10 feet/3 m to the side of the net. He can either shoot from there, to make sure you are hugging the post, or pass to the shooter in front.

If it's a pass, push off the post and centre yourself at the top of the crease before the shot comes. You can't stop a well-aimed shot to either corner while moving (your skateblades can't be turned sideways when you're moving forward).

Showdown

Most goalies love showdowns. Shooters come in on breakaways, and you try to stop them. See if you can stop them more often than they can score.

Movement drills

Staying in the game means knowing the game situation and watching what's going on around you. You see more of the ice than anyone on your team, so help your teammates out: tell them when they're in trouble, or when they have lots of time to make the play.

Goalie Grant Fuhr says that it takes two mistakes to allow a goal. One of those two mistakes is always made by the netminder. Shoulder your part of the responsibility.

Also, you are the only one who's on the ice all the time. So be a leader. Set an example. Give credit when things go right, take responsibility when things go wrong.

One more thing. Be cool.

T H E

GAME

The odd-even rule

When your opponents cross the blueline in front of you, check first to see if your defense is outnumbered.

If it's three-on-three, or any other equal number, come well out to the top of the crease and face the shooter. With the teams at even strength in your zone, a pass is less likely.

If your team is outnumbered and the opposition has an odd man, consider the pass. Come out only to the edge of the crease.

Stepping into the line of fire

Stay alert by moving with the puck, even when it is deep in the other end of the ice. Move sideways and in and out; imagine that you and the puck are connected. Relax, but keep your eyes on the puck. To keep his edge, John Vanbiesbrouck concentrates on the puck even during stoppages in play.

Into your zone

Here the defender is outnumbered. Take the shooter but be ready for a pass. Don't come out too far.

Make sure it's a shootaround before you leave the net.

Move out past the crease and into your crouch or ready position when your opponents bring the puck across the centre redline. But don't root yourself to the spot. Not just yet.

Look for the puck carrier to shoot the puck around your endboards as soon as the centre line is crossed. Only by anticipating the shootaround can you get behind the net fast enough to stop it for your defense.

Handling shootarounds

Your opponents can be out of your zone as fast as they came in if you handle dump-ins right.

Try to field the puck by skating behind the net on the side the puck is shot from. Return by the same side. This helps your defense avoid running into you.

As you turn to go behind your net, watch the puck as it skips around the corner toward you. If the ice is rough at the base of the corner boards, the puck can be deflected in front of your net. Be careful.

Look both ways as you move behind the net. If an opponent is likely to arrive, move the puck yourself. Get it as high on the glass as you can.

When you field the puck from your stick side, face the backboards and stop the puck with the back side of your stick.

TIP

When you're not in the net at practice, carry a puck with you. Work on the same stickhandling and shooting skills your teammates are practising.

Low right side, right-handed goalie: trap the puck with your stick.

High on the boards: get your body on the wall to control the puck.

Left side: easy for a right-handed goalie. Leave the puck away from the boards.

Shootarounds

You can seal off the backboards better from your glove side— on that side you can set your body against the wall and set the toe of your stick against the ice-level dasher. Leave the puck 12 inches/30 cm or so from the dasher.

A word of warning: Make sure it's a shootaround before you leave your net. Don't cheat by leaving early. Better to miss the dump-in than have a shooter in front and you out of the net.

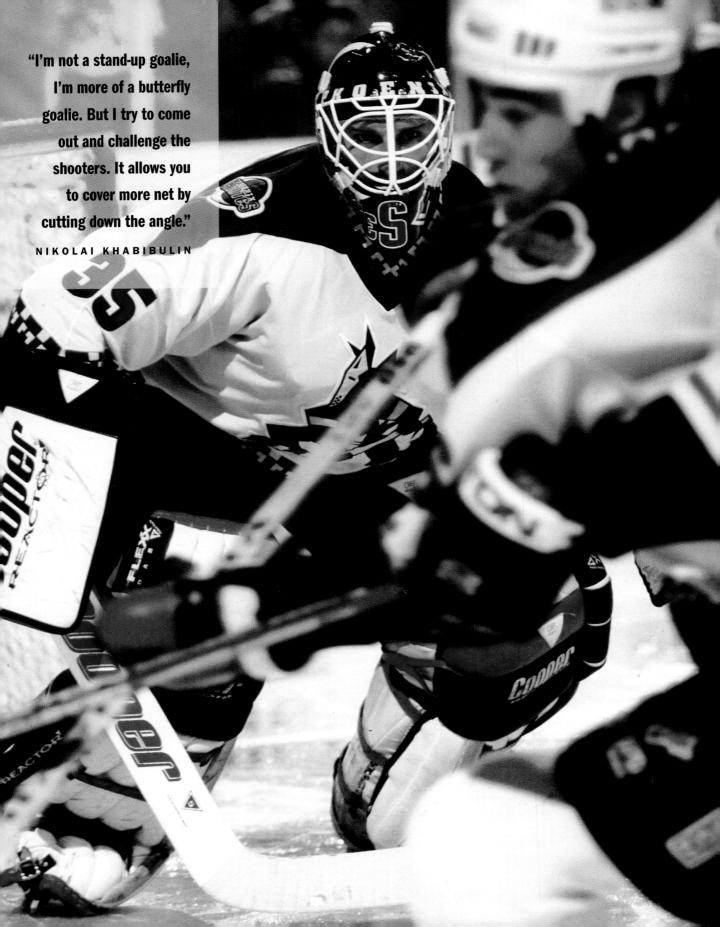

"I'm not a stand-up goalie, I'm more of a butterfly goalie. But I try to come out and challenge the shooters. It allows you to cover more net by cutting down the angle."

NIKOLAI KHABIBULIN

Two-on-one

Call it out to the defense: *"Two*-on-one."

Two things can happen. The puck carrier can shoot or pass. You cover the shot. Your defense is watching for the pass. If the shooter shows signs of wanting to pass, fine. But you are committed to the shooter as long as that player has the puck and is moving toward the net. Don't anticipate, but be aware of the open player.

As soon as the puck carrier passes, react. What you do depends on how close the pass receiver is.

Far out: If the pass is far out of your reach, T-push across, staying on your feet.

In close: If the puck is in close, you may be able to deflect the pass. If not, stack your pads: slide feet-first to the far post.

> **T I P**
> Always commit to the shooter and stay with the shot. Getting the shooter to pass gives your opponents a chance to mess up the play.

On a two-on-one rush, the goalie plays the shooter. Leave the pass to the defender . . .

. . . until the other attacker has the puck. Try to come across on your feet—if possible.

On the rush

If the pass is in close, try to kick out with your lower leg pad before that player can redirect the puck. Don't think about it. Stacking your pads is an instinctive, split-second reaction.

Three-on-one

Make sure it *is* a three-on-one. Is somebody getting back to cancel part of the advantage? If not, call it out. Play deep in your net. Play the shooter, but not as aggressively. Respond to a pass as you would to a two-on-one, but stay on your feet.

Breakaways

All the pressure is on the shooter. This is a read-and-react situation for the netminder. An early clue is where the shooter is carrying the puck. Is the puck to the side or in front? Side means shot. Front means deke.

First, think shot. Be well out beyond the crease and in line with the puck. Take away the shot. You want the shooter to deke. If there is an angle, the closer the shooter gets the more you play the forehand shot. Watch for the defense coming back: they can take one side away from the puck carrier.

Once the shooter comes into the 10-foot/3-m zone stick-handling with the puck in front, it's a deke. Now you have the edge. Hold your ground. Don't go for the deke. Make the puck carrier commit to one side or the other.

Breakaways

Be well out of the net to take away the shot, but not too far to get back in . . .

The puck carrier is coasting in shooting position. Hold your ground . . .

The shooter decides to deke. Wait for him or her to commit, then react.

Once the puck carrier has committed to one side, don't overreact. Often your opponent will tuck the puck under you as soon as you open your legs. Keep your stickblade on the ice and between your legs. Depending on your style, play the move with your pad or skateblade. Keep your glove ready for the flip shot.

The key in moving to one side or the other on a deke is to get the pad on that side down fast. And if you can get your pad down and then kick out, that's even better. Making the breakaway save can turn a game around. Nothing feels better.

"Goaltending coach Ian Young stresses skating. He says you don't have to be a great skater but you have to be a strong skater. I worked a lot on my skating ability to try and improve."

JEFF HACKETT

Point shots

How you play a point shot depends on what is going on around you. An unchecked opponent to your side forces you back into your net, to guard the back door. An unchecked opponent in front of you forces you to get as close as possible behind that player, to smother the deflection.

Remember, once your opponents are established in your zone—as in a power play—read the play. Try to stay on your feet. Let the puck play you.

Faceoffs in your zone

Be ready for anything. How is your centre doing on draws? If the opposing centre has a forehand shot toward you, beware of a shot right off the drop.

In your zone

Be well out for a point shot. Take away as much net as possible . . .

. . . until another opponent appears. You still play the shot, but cheat back into your net. Don't let that open player get behind you for the easy tip-in.

Most often, the opposing centre will try to draw the puck back to a shooter near the slot. How the centre holds a stick tells you a lot.
- Reversed lower hand = draw back.
- Normal grip + forehand toward you = shot.

Check your equipment during the pause. Make sure your foot straps aren't loose. Let the official know if you're not ready. Look at the centre before the puck drops to see which way he or she shoots. Make sure your centre checks with you before committing to the faceoff. Then focus—totally—on the drop of the puck.

Wraparounds

When your opponents have possession behind your net, keep your stance. Do not turn around. Look back over your shoulders.

To get to the opposite post, T-push across in one push off the near post, then turn the toe of your lead skate inward so the puck can't be banked in off your skateblade. Move your stick ahead of you and past the far post, but keep the blade open (not parallel to the goal line) on the way across. This will prevent the puck carrier from banking the puck off your stick into the net. Turn your stickblade slightly out from the goalmouth on the way across and then turn it square to the puck carrier once it is outside the post.

Reach ahead with your stick as you move across. You can prevent passouts just by having your stick outside the post before you get there.

T I P
Never leave the post until you lose sight of the puck going the other way.

Kendall is waiting, skateblade against the post, as Will comes around from behind. No chance . . .

. . . so he goes the other way. Kendall is already there, ready to poke-check the puck off his stick.

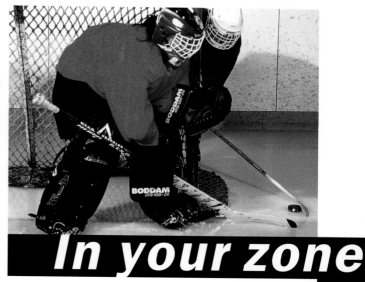

In your zone

In-your-zone checklist

- If you lose sight of the puck, get low. You can see through legs better than through bodies.
- When your team is losing faceoffs in your end, cheat toward the shooter—unless the opposing centre has a forehand shot on you.
- Are your teammates running around after the puck? Be cool. They need you more than ever now.
- Thank your defense for big plays. Nobody else will notice.

Avoiding blocker rebounds

A skill that has almost disappeared from hockey is the art of taking the puck in your catcher after you've stopped it with your blocker.

How to do it

Bring your mitt across, palm up, so the puck can drop into it after it hits your blocker. (You will have eliminated a rebound and can get a faceoff.) The trick is to field the puck with your blocker held vertically. That means getting your elbow up and out front, which is a good idea anyway. Once the puck is in your catching glove, you can keep the puck in play by dropping it where you want it.

If you want to avoid a transfer from glove to glove, let the puck hit your blocker and then smother it with your open catching mitt. Maintain your balance.

Rebounds

Prevent rebounds. Trap the puck on your blocker or let it drop into your catcher. Hold it for a faceoff.

Once you have the puck, get a faceoff by moving toward an opponent near the crease.

Getting a faceoff

Once you've made the save and have the puck in your mitt, you might want to give your team a break. But there is no opponent near you, and the referee is waiting for you to play the puck.

With the puck safe in your catcher, move toward the nearest opposing player. Often, an opponent will skate toward you. That gives you a reason to hold the puck. Most times the referee will call a faceoff instead of the delay-of-game penalty you might have received.

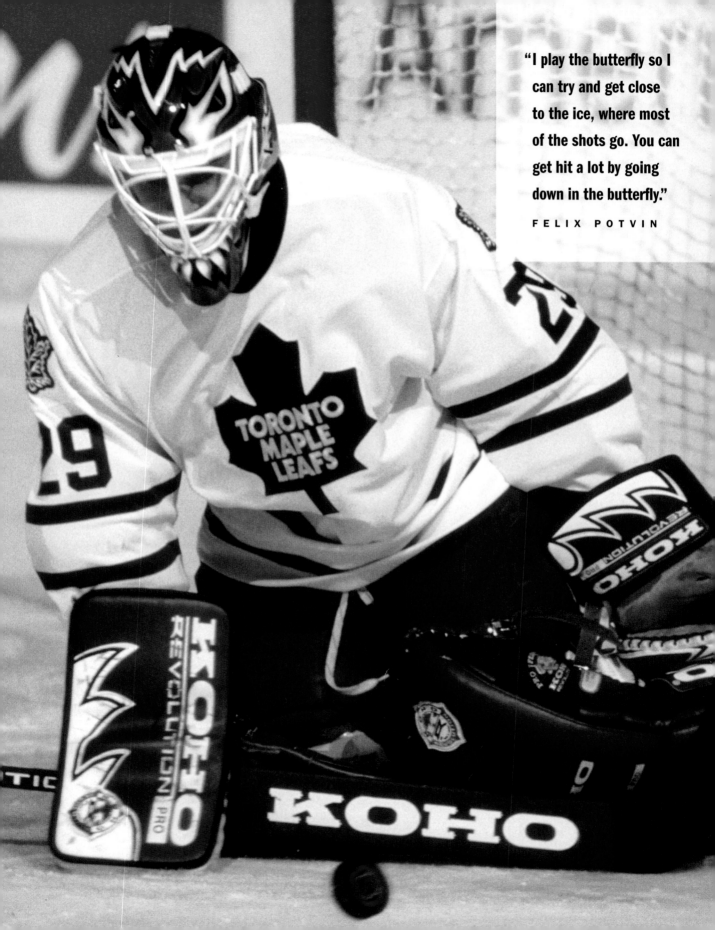

"I play the butterfly so I can try and get close to the ice, where most of the shots go. You can get hit a lot by going down in the butterfly."

FELIX POTVIN

Sean Burke is a big goalie with great reflexes. He handles the puck so well that he outscored seven of his teammates one season.

Be a leader

You are the only player on your team who sees the big picture. Help your teammates when trouble comes knocking, or when there's an opening they don't see. If you help keep your team organized in its own zone, that builds confidence, and it shows that you're in the game. Remember, though, you are yelling through a mask. Keep your message simple and positive. Be urgent, but under control. Never sound panicky.

■ When your teammate has the puck and a checker is coming from the blind side or from behind, yell "*On* you!"
■ When your teammate is double teamed, yell "*Two* to beat!"
■ When a teammate is blocking your view, yell "Screen! Screen!"
■ Call it out when your defense is outnumbered at the blueline. Yell "*Two*-on-one! *Three*-on-one!"

Stay in the game

Don't just give your teammates the bad news.

■ When a teammate has the puck in the open but no idea who might be around, yell "You got *time*!"
■ To a teammate coming back for a loose puck, with his or her back to the play, yell "*No* pressure!"
■ Often your opponents will dump the puck to get a change. Let your teammate know. Yell "They're *chang*ing!"
■ Watch the farthest official, who will call icings. Let your teammate know. Yell "Icing!" or, more important, "*No* call!"
■ Let your team know when its power play is about to expire: bang your stick on the ice when there are five seconds left. Call out the name of the defense player nearest the penalty box.

Communication

Be a good sport

It also pays to communicate with the officials. When they compliment you on a good save, say "Thanks." Let them know you appreciate good calls. Often, they will tell you how they work— and if a referee tells you he or she lets the players play, that's important information.

After the game, communicate with your opponents. Show them respect. Congratulate them. You know better than anyone on your team how good your opponents are. If it was a tight game, they deserve compliments as much as your team does. Shaking hands after the game is a chance to be a good sport.

It will happen. Sooner or later, you will faithfully follow your pregame routine, visualize yourself playing the lights out, work up a healthy sweat in the warmup—and still be stone cold at the drop of the puck. But there are ways of finding out if you're not ready—before the scoreboard tells everyone else.

What to do

- When you feel your upper-body sweat go cold, you've been standing around too long. Give yourself a pep talk. Don't think it, say it. Right out loud. Tell yourself you are asleep. Tell yourself to wake up. Find a two- or three-word piece of advice to repeat to yourself: "Give them nothing!" Or, " Get into it!" What you say is not that important. Saying it over and over is.
- Focus on the puck, wherever it is.
- Keep busy between shots. Check your equipment. Move around the net. Don't worry about looking silly. You'll look sillier fishing the puck out of your net.
- Try to play the puck—and make the right decision—on routine plays. Do the little things right.

The mind game

T I P

Don't dwell on the past. Move on. Be in the present. Your most important save is always the next one.

Game time checklist

- Are you communicating with your defense? If you are in your shell, you are not in the game.
- Have you been lucky so far? The shooters won't be hitting the posts all night.
- Are you aware of the time on the clock?
- Are you just standing around while the puck is in the other end, or are you keeping busy?

The puck is in the net

How you react to being scored on can make or break you as a goaltender. Remember, even the best goaltenders give up an average of one goal for every 10 shots. The trick is to make the next save. It helps to note how the goal was scored. Think for a moment how you might have played it differently, and then park those thoughts. Seal them off.

The single most important mental habit a goaltender can develop is to admit failure, learn from it and move on. The past is history, the future is a mystery and the present is a gift.

"When I go into the butterfly, I like to have my gloves higher. When my arms are in the right position, I know my stickblade is flat on the ice."

PATRICK ROY

Nobody will tell you this, but almost all goalies buy their equipment for the way it looks, rather than for how it works. The great Russian goalie Vladislav Tretiak, for example, took up hockey because he liked the uniforms.

A goalie's equipment is part of his or her style and personality. Leg pads are made differently for stand-up or butterfly goalies. But all goalie equipment has to fit right in order to protect.

Goaltending equipment is expensive. It deserves care. One characteristic of good goalies is the way they care for their equipment. For goalies, more than most athletes, equipment that's cared for is equipment that takes cares of you.

E Q U

DOMINIK HASEK ▶

P M E N T

Goalie sticks are so light and durable that you only need to think about two things when choosing one: the size of your wallet, and does it have the right lie?

The right lie

The lie of a stick is the angle at which the blade meets the shaft. The lower the lie number, the more shallow the angle of shaft to blade. For most goalies, the rule is: The shorter the goalie, the lower the lie. A low lie, such as a No. 13, is closer to that of other hockey sticks, and is better for handling and shooting the puck. The disadvantage is that it leaves a wider opening along the ice between the heel of the stick and the stick-side skateblade when the goalie is in the ready position.

Choosing a stick

As you learn to shoot, try a stick with a lower lie.

A stand-up goalie needs a higher lie . . .

. . . while a butterfly goalie needs a lower lie than Brandon has here.

T I P

Buy skates that fit. Don't buy skates bigger than your size, hoping you'll grow into them.

Curved or straight?

Younger and beginning goalies should stick to straight-blade sticks for three reasons:

- You don't yet have the strength to shoot the puck high on the glass, the main advantage of a curved blade.
- A curved blade tends to direct rebounds in front of the net, rather than to the sides.
- A shorter goalie will have trouble keeping the entire length of a curved stickblade on the ice.

Skates

Goalie skates come in two types: plastic shell with booties, and leather uppers with plastic reinforcements.

For hard-to-fit feet, the shell type offers the most flexibility. Some goalies also feel they offer better protection—and they last. Replace the booties, you've got new skates. Skates with leather uppers require a longer break-in period. But in the long run, for a standard foot, the break-in period will pay off in a better fit.

Leg pads

Leg pads come in all sizes and shapes, with different styles for stand-up or butterfly goalies. Stand-up goalies use shorter pads. Pads for butterfly goalies wrap more padding inside the knees.

Kendall's pads have extra protection inside the knees.

Store your pads with the wettest part up, so they'll dry faster. The pros do.

These older pads are worn away inside the toes. Avoid this.

Skates & pads

Look your pads over after every use. Use a good moisture repellant, especially around the foot area and down the inside of the pad, where a butterfly goalie's pads meet the ice. Moisture adds weight to pads. Store your pads upside down so they hold their shape and the wettest parts dry fastest; the pros do.

Check your toe straps. Keep spares in your bag. Wrap tape around the middle of the toe strap to cushion impacts. Do the same at the point where the first (or first two) bottom-foot strap rubs on the skateblade supports.

Trapper (catching mitt)

Your catching mitt is your most personal piece of equipment. It makes saves all by itself and seldom gives up rebounds. Why not give it some extra care? After games, stack four pucks in the pocket and wrap an elastic-velcro shinguard strap around it to deepen the pocket. Don't just toss it in your bag.

Blocker

About all you have to worry about with a blocker is wearing holes in the inner fingers. Small holes actually help you grip the stick, but once they get larger, a bare finger on your stick is an invitation to a permanent disability. Get the holes fixed.

Mitts & masks

Look for stiffness along the thumb and wrist guard of a used catching mitt.

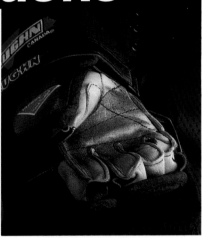

Used blockers are fine if the glove palm is fully intact.

Michelle's goal mask and throat protector overlap, leaving no openings.

Helmet/mask

This is one item where you can save money. Not every goalie needs a custom-painted pro-style mask. A helmet/cage combination can get the job done for about half the cost of a pro-style Fiberglas cage combination. Make sure all the screws and fasteners are tight before every game.

If you use a helmet/cage model, look for a cage with square, rather than rounded, bars and openings. Andy Moog says that a little extra padding in the sides and back doesn't hurt in making a slightly oversize—but CSA-approved—unit fit better.

It costs a lot of money to buy goaltending equipment, and a sure sign of a good goalie is how he or she takes care of it. Your gear spends a lot of time in your bag, so bag it right.

Packing your bag needs to become a routine, with everything going into its place. That way, if something is missing, you'll know right away. (If your skates go inside your bag, use skate guards to protect your other gear.)

Keep some spares on hand: toe straps, helmet fasteners, tape and an extra pair of socks. An oily rag in a zip-lock bag is ideal for cleaning off skateblades. On top of everything else, buy yourself a carpet sample. For a couple of bucks, you get your own mobile, carpeted dressing room stall.

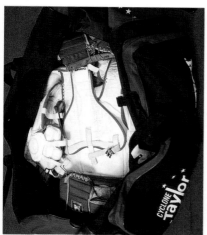

Figure out a good way to pack your equipment, and stick with it . . .

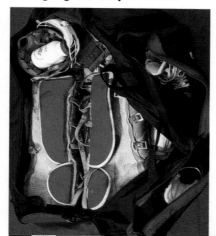

. . . so you'll notice if something is missing. A goalie really hates that.

Build strong off-ice routines. The games are crazy enough.

Packing your bag

Of course, everything must come out between games. Set your equipment out to dry as soon as you return home. Make yourself do it every time. This is a good habit to develop, and it is one of the few times when you can think about how well you played.

If you won, try to think of something you learned. If you lost, try to find something you did right. Finally, what was the best moment of all? Remember that big save as you set your equipment out to dry, checking it for wear or damage. Give yourself credit. Be your own coach.

Goalies might not skate long distances, but leg strength and power are as important as with any other player. Maybe more so. You are moving up and down and sideways, changing direction and skating in bursts—and doing most of it as quickly as possible.

Some goalies don't take conditioning seriously. But the best ones do. Patrick Roy rides a stationary bike and does easy jogging when he has the chance. Mike Richter warms up for games by running laps around the loading zones of arenas. Ed Belfour does dry-land workouts to build flexibility and thigh- and lower-back strength. Kelly Hrudey often stretches during games, and does the splits in his net during delays.

Working out helps keep them all in the NHL.

F I T

CHRIS OSGOOD

N   E   S   S

Guy Hebert is a big-save goalie—at his best when the other team peppers his net. His angles have improved: he covers the low net, challenging shooters to go high on him.

Adding power

If you are between the ages of 8 and 12, don't lift weights. Your muscles and connective tissues are still growing. If you injure them by lifting weights, you will have serious health problems. Grant Fuhr says that "a goaltender must be agile, not musclebound." Still, exercises that use your own body mass to build power can't hurt.

Push-ups: Keep yourself honest—keep your back straight.

Sit-ups/abdominal crunches: These help goalies return quickly to their feet after going down, and build support for the back muscles.

Squats: A must for goalies. Billy Smith, who won four Stanley Cups with the Islanders, could do sets of 40 in under a minute.

Legs as wide apart as possible. Back straight. Lean forward. Feel the strain.

You'll feel this in your lower back on your bent-leg side. Pull on your other foot.

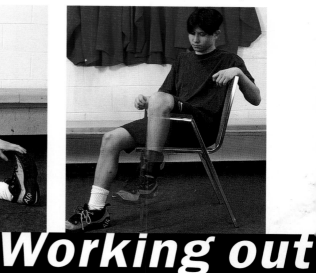

With a 2-pound/1-kg ankle weight, swing leg straight. Do sets of five, each leg.

Working out

Stretching

You can't play goal without being flexible. You have to balance strength with stretching, not only to avoid or minimize injuries, but to tone the muscles you build with exercise.

The stretches shown here concentrate on the groin muscles, quadriceps, hamstrings and the lower back.

Coordination & awareness

Many goaltending coaches recommend that goalies play table tennis, to improve their hand-eye coordination. Good peripheral vision—the ability to see to either side without turning your head or eyes—is also important. To improve your peripheral vision, practise making yourself see things without looking at them.

Resources

Books

Ian Young, whose promising goaltending career was ended by injury, is one of the leading goaltending coaches in the game. His students include Kirk McLean, Jeff Hackett, Felix Potvin, Kelly Hrudey and Mike Fountain. Young has written three good books for young goalies:

Behind the Mask: The Ian Young Goaltending Method
Ian Young and Chris Gudgeon. Polestar Press, Vancouver, 1992.

Beyond the Mask: The Ian Young Goaltending Method, Advanced Techniques
Ian Young and Chris Gudgeon. Polestar Press, Vancouver, 1993.

Lords of the Rink
Ian Young and Terry Walker. Polestar Press, Vancouver, 1994.

Also recommended:

Fuhr on Goaltending
Grant Fuhr with Bob Mummery. Polestar Press, Vancouver, 1988.

Videos

The Puck Stops Here
Jim Park, 1986.
A comprehensive skills digest.

Goaltending Today
International Hockey Centre of Excellence.

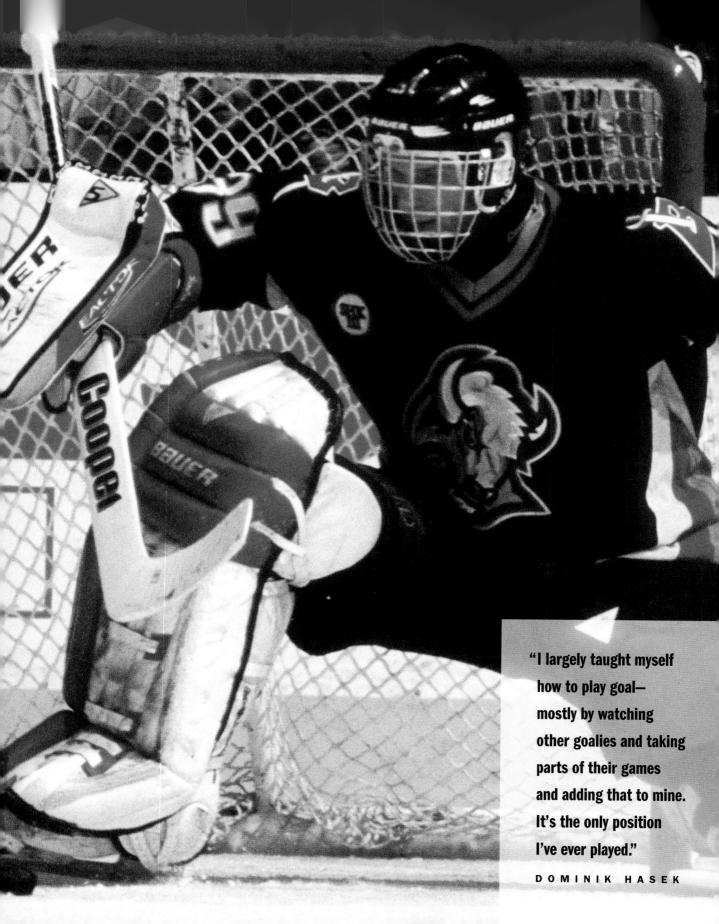

"I largely taught myself
how to play goal—
mostly by watching
other goalies and taking
parts of their games
and adding that to mine.
It's the only position
I've ever played."

DOMINIK HASEK

Photo credits

Photography by Stefan Schulhof/Schulhof Photography, except as indicated below:

Photos by Bruce Bennett Studios:
Front cover: John Giamundo
Back cover & title page spread (Curtis Joseph): p. 8 (background), p. 9: John Tremmel
Back cover & title page spread (Ed Belfour): p. 14 (background), p. 15, p. 59: John Giamundo
Back cover & title page spread (Martin Brodeur, Dominik Hasek), p. 26 (background), p. 27, p. 48 (background), p. 49: Claus Andersen
Back cover & title page spread (Mike Richter), p. 1 (background), pp. 20–21, p. 32 (background), p. 33, p. 44: Scott Levy
Back cover & title page spread (Chris Osgood), p. 54 (background), p. 55: Michael Digirolamo
p. 4: Richard Lewis
p. 7, p. 39: Jim McIsaac
p. 10, p. 36, p. 56: Bruce Bennett
p. 16: Jim Leary
p. 30: Layne Murdoch

Photo by Jack Murray, Kallberg/Darch Studio: p. 25

Photos by Doug MacLellan/Hockey Hall of Fame: p. 43, p. 47

Photo of Brian Burke on p. 5 courtesy of the NHL